A

Past

Left

Unkept

Aketre Whitaker

A Past Left Unkept

Copyright © 2019 by Aketre Whitaker

All rights reserved

ISBN: 9781704055916

Dedication 🕊

    A Past Left Unkept is dedicated to the only granddaddy I've known and spent quality time with, Robert Lee Cooper. I love this man because he was my pure happiness and everything. As a young girl, when I didn't fully understand the "darkness", he was and still is the only light that I remember without a doubt. My granddaddy. When I was five days shy from my 14th birthday on a loud and storming night, God called my granddaddy home. God doesn't make any mistakes; He blessed me with this happiness and light for 14 years. Thank You God for blessing me with such an awesome man that kept me safe and happy in my darkest moments of my life. The pure happiness and love I desired that was gracefully shown by my granddaddy allowed the desire within me to go back to find this light again. Why? So, I can be led back to *A Past Left Unkept* for my healing, deliverance, and being set free. Granddaddy, I did it by God's Grace & Mercy as I dedicate my first book to you. You were and still is the light that allowed me to hold on until I got a chance to know and build an intimate relationship with God for myself, who is forever my light in any dark place.

~~* Love you & Thank you Granddaddy*~*~*

(One of your "A Team" crew members)

Acknowledgments

➤ **God** – Thank You for it all. Thank You for protecting, saving, molding, and everything you've done for me—for being my light in my dark places. Thank You for entrusting me with this vision, and for using me as Your willing vessel. Without You, I'm absolutely nothing; WITH YOU, I AM & HAVE ALL THE RICHES IN THIS WORLD. Nothing else matters—I shall always seek You first in all that I do…Continue ordering my steps Dear Lord, and keeping me humble. To and for You, I will praise and give You ALL the glory, praise, and worship. I love you God!

➤ **My "3" Little Birds—My Kids (Akeonya, Ateonya, & LaDerrick, Jr.)** – You all are the air that I breathe. Times I wanted to throw the towel in; you all gave me strength to carry on, and press through my darkest moments. I love you all to life. Momma, thank you all for loving me while I settled in my mess. Thank you all for always being my #1 cheerleaders. Thank you all for not giving up on me when I made mistakes in life, yet kept pressing to be the best mother I knew how to be. I apologize for any hurt, uncertainty, pain, fear, anger, frustration, etc. that I may have caused during the stage of my life. Please forgive me. Just know this is part of my legacy that I entrust over to you all. If Momma can do it, I know without a shadow of a doubt you all can do it better! Keep God 1st in all that you do, seek His Presence, continue to pray, and when you all cannot seem to get it right; REST IN THE LORD and He will always work it out for your greater good!

➤ **Mother (Cordelia)** – Where do I start Momma? I love you to life. I thank God for having you as my mother. You've been through some things that I probably wouldn't have survived, BUT GOD. Thank you Momma for all that you've poured into me. Thank you for teaching me that obedience, truth, and righteousness were vital aspects of life—Momma, this is what God seeks from us—WOW! Thank you for charging those aspects upon me, so I could get it, yet live it. Thank you Momma. Thank you literally for your unconditional love. Thank you for protecting me the best you knew how. Thank you for helping me raise my kids. Thank you for never turning your back on me. Thank you for being my best friend. Thank you for being the phenomenal, loving, hardworking, humble, righteous, joking, unconditional, strong, and intentional woman you are. I'm proud to say that you're that lady of my life—My Momma!

➤ **Siblings (Anetre, Adarius, Aletre, & Adetre)** – I love you all. I can say that no matter the distance, time away, or what we've been through—we ALWAYS REMEMBER OUR LOVE for each other. Momma taught us to ALWAYS stick together, and we did, and right now are doing just that. We went through so much together, and this is part of you all story too. I pray that God heals your brokenness from your past, and set you all free, deliver, and heal you all because "darkness" is real. If no one else can relate, we can. We can write a book—yeap, here it is. As you all sister, I'm so proud of you all & so thankful to God for you all being my support system. I meant that with my whole heart—We may not always had the most money in the world, yet we have the most valuable and priceless thing---LOVE. Keep pressing & Keep God 1st. I love you all till life.

- ❥ **Nurse (Mozelle Terry)** – Woman of God, you've invested so much into me, all I can do is thank God for you. Nurse Terry, you're such an inspiration, and you saw something in me that I didn't even see myself. The valuable moments you shared, the relentless prayers, the blessings, the invested time—How in the world can I repay you? Thank you for believing in me. I thank God that I have you in my life. You pushed me right into my purpose and professionalism. Even when you didn't or don't say a word, your presence alone brings so much peace. The anointing that you have is so beautiful, and again, I thank God for you. Thank you for it all. Thank you for praying for me when I was so weak, I couldn't even pray for myself. Thank you, thank you, and thank you. I love you!

- ❥ **Leaders/Pastors (Pastor Joyner, Pastor T)** – Thank you all for the awesome teaching of The Word. Thank you for your truth and transparency. Thank you for the covering and guidance you've given me thus far. I thank God for you both, and your true leadership skills that is displayed in your ministries. You both are phenomenal individuals, and thank you for pouring into me, and pushing me to understand the importance of knowing who I am and whose I belong to. Thank you for the relentless prayers, guidance, and unconditional love. Thank you both so much!

➤ **Overseer (Roosevelt Ethridge)** – Thank you for your assistance in my personal and spiritual development. Thank you for your leadership, patience, humility, and unconditional love that is displayed gracefully in and outside the ministry. Thank you for your invested time, prayers, and guidance in the many aspects of life as it relates to serving in and for The Kingdom. The knowledge you've planted in me is phenomenal, yet the life you live in front of everyone is real and so transparent. Just thank you for being who you are. Thank you for it all!

Thank you all for your support as I maneuvered and is maneuvering through my journey, and for being present as God lead me back to A Past Left Unkept!

Table of Contents

Introduction

Have you ever been around something or someone, and it's just something that doesn't feel right, yet life happens, and you must move on? Have you ever been so hurt for so long, so many times, by so many people that you become numb to pain? So numb to the pain that embracing life of sin feels so good that no matter what, it is right? Yet in the same token, life continues to happen no matter what—if you understand it or not; life goes on right?

Wait, what about the desire to keep numbing the pain until one day you find or found yourself in a desperate situation in which you are pleading or pleaded for God to help and save you. Now the debate is happening in your mind: Am I ready to give this lifestyle up for one I'm so uncertain about? You are then faced with your hard truth, yet life is happening and/or happened. You noticed that more, more, and more things are being piled upon you, yet you are pondering continuously in your head about this "darkness" you can't seem to shake. You're screaming in the inside because you're so broken, yet you have to pretend to the world that you have *it all* under control. You've hit rock bottom—no other choice, but to choose God because everything else failed or is failing. Still, you are questioning is this the way you really want to go?

Time to look in the mirror and accept your truth no matter how ugly, painful, happy, sad—IT'S YOURS, and it has to be accepted, either now or later. After you yearn for a resolution, you begin identifying, accepting, acknowledging, and facing your truth. You notice you're seeing things in a different perspective, yet life is still happening. Before you realize it, temptation and the need to go back to that familiar place of numbness, which in the same token is a mental place of comfort begins to resurface. What do you do now?

Another decision that has to be made, yet you've had an encounter or some encounters with God. These encounters with God aren't explainable, yet you know they are real, gives you peace, and a feeling like no other. It feels and tastes good—God is so good! With you knowing this, you've made the decision to go back to that familiar place. You're now feeling a sense of guilt from the life of sin you thought you was finished with and had walked away from. Now realizing you just had to go back to get another taste of it. It literally feels as if your heart is breaking in a million pieces. Why? Not only do you feel as if you've let yourself down, what about God? Do you continue to indulge in it, or press pass the pain to gain an understanding of what that "darkness" is that continues to hoover over you that will not go away? Your choice. What is it going to be?

Depending on your readiness, are you ready to let go and surrender? What if you can't handle your "darkness" when the truth from it comes out? What if your "darkness" ends up being someone or some people you love? What's next? How do you forgive someone you love? In the end, is it really worth going back to a past left unkept?

Grab your blanket, cup of your favorite beverage, get somewhere quiet, and let's see……..

Chapter 1

Being Numb to the Pain

Question: Have you ever been through so much in life, and so much pain be attached to and with it, that it leaves you numb? It's just like walking two miles on concrete with smaller shoes than your actual size, yet you know you must make it to your destination. Even though you feel the pain and numbness, you must continue, and deal with the outcome later, even if it means getting your foot amputated or even getting a new pair of shoes in the end that fits. You never know the outcome until you've pressed passed the pain. Welcome to my life. My childhood remains a blur to me due to me conditioning my mindset to block out the "darkness" of it, yet one thing that highlights as I think back over it, is always resonating with the feeling of being numb to the pain.

This pain centered on being exposed to so much abuse at such a young age---from emotional to mental, from mental to physical, and from physical to being afraid to even tell anyone about it. This was a part of my "darkness" that I knew existed without a shadow of a doubt, yet too fearful to go deeper because so often I remembered how easy it was to feel the pain yet be so numb to it at the same time. Not only that, but knowing "darkness" existed, yet living a life of uncertainty around the unanswered questions of what this "darkness" really was, or even who was this "darkness"? I knew something existed beyond what I remembered, yet what was it? I could feel it, but what was it?

After witnessing some tough things day after day as it related to seeing my mother being beat, hearing her daily pleas through her cries for it to stop, hearing constant belittling towards a woman I truly loved and adored with all of me, not being shown things about life, not knowing what it meant to be a young lady—these things were normal for me, this was my true definition of living, as I thought and lived it to be. I finally realized that I made it day by day through all this dysfunction simply by being numb to the pain. Pain that stemmed so deep that all I wanted to do was leave it all behind and get another life. May I add, that was my only wish that I spoke so many, many, many times. Why? I had become so complacent of being numb to the pain that my life didn't matter if I could press to that numbness in which I found immediate comfort in.

As I recall my childhood, as I reflect, and touch a past left unkept, even at the age of five, I was broken. Broken because the cards that I was dealt at such a young age came with an ultimate cost. I felt as if I had to adapt to the conditions of these tough, ugly, negative, and hurtful cards every day. What other options were available? Where is the nearest safe place? How much can one person take? Help me somebody……

From seeing my mother get abused by men that claimed they loved her, to witness seeing a gun being put to my brother's head as he ran to stop a man from shooting my mother in her head, to hearing a gun going off from a man that tried to force himself in the house yet decided to shoot himself on the side of the house, to seeing men physically attack my oldest sibling when she tried helping our mother--- to being the little girl that so tightly held her sisters and brother's hands with tears rolling down her face so many times while hiding under the bed. My God; I survived the moments simply by being numb to the pain.

Imagine fearing to go to bed at night because you didn't know what the next second would bring. Jumping in your sleep at every loud noise that hit your ear. Crying yourself to sleep because you wanted your life to be free of the violence, but knowing there's nothing you could do, but be afraid and cry. Being the one to always be ready to make sure the house was clean to avoid the torturing beatings and verbal, emotional, and mental abuse from a man that you thought loved you and your mother yet being shown different. At this moment, at the age of eleven, I questioned love, trust, security, and even life. All I knew to do was continue being numb to the pain.

Before I could realize that my normalization of being numb to the pain became a routine of adaptation, I was looking in the mirror at a so broken teenager getting ready to head to high school. What am I supposed to do about relationships? Why am I fearing other people? Why can't I trust anyone? What am I to do when and if someone violates me? All these questions filled my head because my mother was so busy protecting us that I never thought to ask her how to face reality—my life and the real world. All I knew was how to avoid anything by being numb to the pain….Did that really matter now since life happened, and it was time for me to put all that I knew to work as it related to surviving in the real world? I thought on many occasions that it would be easier than the abuse I saw, yet was I setting myself up for failure, or was I really preparing myself to rest in the comfort of being numb to the unforeseen pain that could possibly lie

ahead?

Chapter 2

Life Happens

Well, here I am a freshman in high school, still pure as I reference my virginity, yet surrounded by so many people— males. Anxiety, frustration, fear, happiness, and uncertainty instantly filled my entire composition or being. What am I to do? Is this place appropriate for me to hide behind the numbness of my pain? Well, life happens, and it happened. First relationship at high school was with a male that was almost five or six years older than me which was an experience. I loved the fact that the older guy chose me of course because in my head I thought I was doing something. Was I really? Did I know what I was putting myself in? Was I ready and prepared for what happened next?

After about two months, I started to see the "exact" things that I witnessed seeing my mother go through—the belittling, the verbal, emotional, and mental abuse—and then I found myself laying on my boyfriend's bed being choked out, and forcibly being penetrated as he looked in my eyes to tell me he loved me. Tears rolled down my face as I internally called my mother to help me in such a vulnerable and helpless state. By no means did I want that sexual exchange, yet instantly I remembered I could find comfort in it by being numb to the pain. I remember going home that day, and literally sitting in the corner rocking back and forth with my head buried in my knees with my tears soaking my pants. Vividly remembering the sense of "darkness" upon me real heavy as I asked myself why does this feel so familiar all of a sudden—this "darkness"?

Life happened, and it was not fair to me because it reflected all that I went through as a young girl. Well, I stayed in the relationship until I received my last busted lip. I tried hiding it because I realized that this guy I considered as my boyfriend really was an abuser, jealous, and very opposite of what I thought I would have. Yet instead, it was simply a reflection of what I had been through and came as

A Past Left Unkept

familiar with as a young girl growing up, adapting to, and being molding by dysfunction. Thank God for His Grace and Mercy as I reflect because He saved me. Thank You Lord. I instantly begun having trust issues.

I became focused on my studies, and really didn't focus on being in a relationship, yet I still had a special place for this guy that just blew me off my feet since middle school that I saw roaming the hallways every day, Paul. Paul became my safe haven per se that I'd searched for all my life. He did not make me feel the way that the other guy made me feel; he didn't look like what I witnessed at home as a young girl; he was "the one". Paul and I were friends, lovers, and homies---our bond was unexplainable because we always kept our friendship, yet relationship was on and off. So during our off period, life happened, and I became pregnant at the age of fifteen. Yes, a baby having a baby; the constant stares, the negative talks, the laughs, the whispers, the feeling of shame—all of that I faced, BUT GOD!

21

So, within 7 months of my pregnancy, the same cycle begun to surface again—Guess what? The twenty calls back to back, the stalking, and the straw that broke the camel's back—the guy that I was pregnant by, literally pushed me down the steps. At that moment I knew, I couldn't and wasn't going through the abuse again. If I couldn't do it for myself, I knew I had to do it for my unborn child. That relationship ended—BUT GOD! Paul was still there, and always was supportive, so I had a support system. Paul was the one that I truly loved!

Here was this broken girl, now the mother of a beautiful daughter, uprising Junior in high school, academically gifted—now at a point of realization that life was happening and had happened. Even though life happened, I possessed the desire to still persevere, press, and finish school; I knew I needed a sound and concrete plan—I'm a mother. So therefore, I took classes that I knew would benefit me and my daughter after graduation. I did just that—graduated with honors and received my certification and license as a

Certified Nursing Assistant (CNA). Now realized at that

moment, education was still a must—yet being a mother that

was present was most important. I turned down scholarships

to attend a local college, so I could raise my daughter. Even

though my mother was willing to raise her, which she helped

me out so much, I knew I had to be accountable, and my

daughter was my responsibility. Boy, this was tough, yet I

had to do what I had to do because I had a mouth to feed and

had to be a positive role model to my little one.

I went to college, and yet again, in my sophomore year, I

became pregnant now with my second child. Life was

happening; Life happened. Now I was excited because with

my child's father this time, we decided to do things the right

way to raise our family together, so we got married. Now

here I was married at the age of twenty-four with two

children—educated and determined, yet still broken as I

feared the surfacing of this "darkness". As I looked around

one night as my family slept, I remember saying to myself: 'What am I to do now, momma never taught me how to prepare for this life I have—how to be a mother and wife.' I remembered being so terrified by the thoughts of failing, I cried myself to sleep on the sofa to wake up to my husband holding me. Life happened. My marriage became tough, trials, and tribulations, but guess what--- I'm starting to see small signs of my past surfacing when I recalled being that little girl that was so terrified. I just remembered the "darkness in the corner" brought comfort because I was numbed to the pain.

Alcohol played a part of the reason why those men beat my mother, yet now I was looking in and at the same mirror in my own marriage. As I reflect on it, mentally for me, alcohol was my husband's lover that I felt the need to compete with; not knowing the whole time, I was already defeated. The man that was my lover, homie, and best friend—now my husband—was starting to look just like the men that I feared when I was a little girl. Now, not only did I have to protect myself and my two children; I found out I had to protect another one. I was now pregnant again with my third child.

Life happened. A mother of three at the age of twenty-six, married to a man that I loved for so long, yet was at a place and point of uncertainty in life. Why? Now not only was alcohol the lover, more lovers came—adultery, deceit, and lies. These lovers were replacing my position in his life as his wife. I dealt with and faced so many internal debates mentally as to what to do; the main one was whether I stay to make it work or leave to save me and my kids. Of course, coming from a broken and traumatic childhood, I wanted my family to stay together because I never had this. At that moment, my husband and I were going to fight through our tough moments and try to put all the negative things behind us. It took more extreme pain, headaches, heartbreaks, disrespect, and bruises for me to wake up per se.

I finally realized that I could not fight the *many lovers* or be in a dilemma of him choosing between the many—not being his wife and the mother of his children. Not only this, it went from the verbal attacks to holding a pool of blood that ran from my face due to his drunkenness of busting a beer bottle in my face, to being hit in the back of the head with the bunt of a gun, to dropping on my knees looking at him in his eyes pleading for him to just kill me. It not only left me emotionally and mentally scarred; even today, as I look in the mirror, the physical scars are still present and will be until I leave this world. More brokenness on top of brokenness at this point.

I knew it would be better to separate than to stay together at this point; it wasn't worth it. I was willing to face the shame, the struggles, the silent whispers, the fact that I was possibly about to raise three kids alone. I was prepared to deal with that than the continuous abuse that was tearing me down in totality day by day. I thought if I continued to allow

that, I may just be dead for real, and then my kids will be
without a mother. So now, so much was channeling in my
mind, I noticed that my husband's reactions, behaviors, and
disposition changed. It went from hey phatty bread
(nickname he gave me) to no communication, hugging me to
no affection at all, understanding to increased arguing for no
reason at all, being open about everything to the hiding of
the cell phone, and to coming home at a decent time to
coming in late at night with no explanation at all. All I knew
to do as a wife was to accept it and keep taking care of my
kids and home. As if it was yesterday, I vividly remember
when we moved to our new beautiful home—the best we
have ever had. I was excited now relieved because this meant
a new beginning. Was it really?

I thought! The first day at our new beautiful home, his
phone rung in the back where I was; he was upfront. I
answered the phone filling my heartbeat race so fast, it
literally felt like someone pounding on a drum. I became

nervous suddenly. Then I heard the voice on the other end, and she said, "I'm *Sally*, I'm the one who's been sleeping with your husband, I finally get to hear your voice to tell you that, just because you moved in that pretty house doesn't mean anything, I guarantee you, he won't be staying there tonight." The call became disconnected. This woman never knew that she added on to the brokenness that already existed within from what my husband was showing me, yet the truth that I wasn't prepared to accept. My husband had a mistress. My heart instantly crumbled in a million and one pieces filled with tears, hurt, pain, agony, lost, loneliness, disloyalty, and distrust that covered them. I went numb to the pain, yet having to pull it together for my kids, I continued with what I was doing before the call as if that call never happened. Life was happening. Life happened!

I cried silently within and continued to unpack the boxes, smiled pass the pain—conditioned myself to be numb to the pain, and got my kids settled in our new beautiful home.

Meanwhile, mind toggling questions immediately happen at the speed of a jet: How did she even know we'd moved? What have he told this woman about me? Does he really love her or is it a sex thing? How long has this been going on? Does my husband really love me? Is he leaving tonight? What if, he leaves, what am I supposed to do? Why would he do this to me? Why did he have to go out to cheat versus just talking about it? Is my marriage over? What can I do to make it work? What if he leaves me to go be with this woman? What about our kids? Can I do this alone? Yes, it seemed like a million questions filled my head all at once. Then I snapped out of this question zone when I began to hear what? Guess what? An out of the blue argument happening for no apparent reason at all. For the first time out of my 7-year marriage, my husband left and did not come home. This woman was right; he didn't stay home during our first night in our new beautiful home.

Now, I had to suck all the emotions and feelings up that came with this and protect my kids. Our kids asked questions, yet being a woman who lived in the abuse, became numbed to so much pain—I had to lie to my children to protect their hearts, so they wouldn't learn how to become numb to their pain. Also, so they wouldn't know that their mother at that moment felt like a failure, was being abused, yet struggling to face her current moment and reality of abandonment and rejection. I was supposed to know how to keep my husband home, yet instantly, I went back to the "darkness" of comfort, and yet again….I pressed through the fact that I may be facing a divorce, yet I was okay because I had already numbed myself to the situation, nevertheless, to the pain. Why was the familiarity of this "darkness" still hovering over me?

Chapter 3

Embracing the Life of Sin

As I embraced life as it was---falling to pieces—facing divorce, being a single-parent, facing shame, and dealing with the pain; I needed HELP! I wasn't ready to accept the fact that all of this was happening at my own front door. I found comfort in alcohol, sex, partying, and deceit. To the world, I had to portray that my life was still perfect. I put on the fake smile, kept myself up in terms of hair dos, expensive cars, nice clothes, and had it going on per se. Yet, no one really ever knowing that this man that I called my husband had abused me, and still yet, I was so broken and a complete mess on the inside.

Reality set in, it was just me and my three kids. I still played my part and functioned as a mother—nothing to me at that moment lacked because I was doing my job as a mother. When I made sure that my kids were good, I went out to have fun. My fun looked like going out to the clubs, drinking alcohol, having orgies with females, and being with men—three married and one wasn't. My kids never knew my lifestyle that was derived and rooted from all this pain. There wasn't a desire to stop this madness because I knew that the woman's voice, I heard was the same woman that my husband left me and my kids for. At that moment, I was going through that pain and shame on top of that in which I endured. Lust became an ultimate desire that I needed to release my pain. At that moment in my life, all I desired was for the voids to be filled—sex and alcohol. I practiced safe sex because even though my life was so black and corrupt, I knew I had to live for my kids. Instead of being numb to the pain, I now embraced the life of sin especially sex and alcohol.

When it came to sex, it came a point in which I desired women versus men. I dealt with men occasionally, yet that thing for a woman I desired more than anything. It was so mentally real for me to have a woman that the thought of one would arouse me to a climax even when sitting at work, home, or out in public. Yes, it was that real and desirable for me. Since I had fulfilled my fantasy of being with a woman, I needed more. It was times in which, I would leave late at night, meet my female lover down a path just to feel her touch. I had to have it. After a while, I realized that being intimate with women had become an addiction. It took me back to my marriage when I saw my husband desiring the need of alcohol, and then I had to pause to think about this desire. I knew that I was enjoying the intimacy of being with a woman, yet never thought of what I was creating in that woman or the women I dealt with. It became so normal, and a part of my life that I had a couple of women tell me that they were in love with me. I knew my sexual aspect and performance was alright, yet not to have another woman tell me that. I evaluated myself and knew that was not my ultimate goal of falling in love or a relationship; I became scared, and fell back from the engagements. Immediately, I didn't want them to feel the pain I felt when my husband left me, so I had to give them my truth of not wanting to continue on with that lifestyle. I could not be that woman for them any longer.

Even though at that moment, I gave them my truth, I still was dipping and dabbing every now and then, yet I knew life couldn't go on this way. I had to get a grip on what really mattered, and that was me needing to heal, yet being present for my kids even in my brokenness and embracement of exotic sin. Now, I had to face my truth and reality---I had to cope to a life that once was filled with everything I desired, yet my truth had me to face the fact that it was over.

It was over, and I had to move pass it the best I knew how. I remember sitting on my bed getting ready to pick up that gin bottle, dropping it, and screaming out to God to help me.

THE MOMENT THAT CHANGED MY LIFE!

I remembered the Serenity Prayer—God grant me the serenity to accept the things I cannot change; courage to change the things I can, and the wisdom to know the difference. Courage and wisdom came, and I knew that I could no longer embrace the life of sin yet embracing and getting to know God had to be the way. As soon as I let God in to help me cope with, understand, and live beyond my broken marriage, the alcohol, and sex—something began to happen. Peace came over me, and I was finally facing my realities of life. That moment I now know, God was getting ready to take me through my process---transformation.

Before I could go any further, God told me that I had to accept my truth. The truth required an act of obedience, fully trusting God with my process, and knowing who I was beyond the brokenness and embracement of sin. So many questions filled my heart and mind. I began asking God: Are you sure you can clean this drunken and sexual woman up? How can you love me when I'm so useless and nasty? What

.

do I have to do to get cleaned up? These questions filled me, and God gently worked with me in lieu of me accepting my truth, as I went through a transformation process. So, so, so hard to accept, definitely not easy, still a work in progress, yet I knew I was doing too much and needed to change. All it took was for me to learn how to accept my truth, confess, repent, and SURRENDER IT ALL to God.

Not dipping and dabbing in and out of the exotic sin yet surrendering the temptation of it was necessary. I thought I could find comfort in it still by embracing a partial of it, yet not realizing that it took me further in a dark place. That dark place did not feel or look good. I was losing more than I was gaining. I could not hear or feel God's Presence. I knew partially dipping and dabbing was not the way or answer. I needed God's Guidance; I could not survive that dark place; I couldn't. Something had to change or happen immediately! The moment that I told God that I truly desired a change, needed a change, and did not want another taste of a female, things truly began to happen in my transformation. It was like the moment that I made up my mind completely that I was tired of being sick and tired of myself, it was time for me to take on the accountability of my truth that I was a weak vessel of flesh, God stepped in and done the rest....

Chapter 4

Accepting My Truth & Transformation

God, my truth! What really is my truth? I began to converse with God at this moment as if I was talking with my mother or someone close to my heart. I was forming an intimate relationship with God. Looking back at this moment, I do not recall God responding to my question. Time after time, I'm like what's really happening—I couldn't hear or feel the presence of God. I immediately done a quick self-evaluation. I knew why I didn't hear from or didn't feel God's Presence. Why? I was still dipping and dabbing in my mess, and not truly accepting my whole and ugly truth in its entirety. My truth was the mere fact that my marriage was over, I deserved so much better in terms of understanding, patience, and love, yet I was so **broken**. Why me God when I've done my best? To cope, I was still living and embracing the life of sin and making commitments that I weren't ready to keep. The power of deceit was my truth. At this point, I didn't care about how others felt, I was hurt, and so at that time, me hurting others was okay with me. I was cold-hearted to a certain degree—not good, yet that was my truth at this stage in my life. I thought I would be better by now, yet and my truth, I was not! I was still hurting!

I began to look at my life as a difficult task to accomplish because in all actuality, I wanted my family back. All this mess was just too much, and I needed my husband back— that one that was my homie, lover, and best friend. I couldn't continue to bear the thoughts of people looking at me, whispering and asking me what happened. It's not like I was able to tell them the truth because I wasn't in a healthy place to talk about it. Nevertheless, to accept the truth of and behind it. My truth hurt me so bad that I chose not to touch it, yet instead moved on with life. Life happened, and yet again, I became numb to the pain. That was my life for years—divorce happened, struggle became real, situationships happened---and as I looked around my three kids were older now as they watched my every move. I felt and faced embarrassment and shame because I knew my oldest two saw my life twirling down and the struggles, yet they still loved their mother—ol' broken me.

When I got sho' nuff tired of secretly hiding my pain because this was starting to spill over to and affecting my relationship with my children; I sought to be in the presence of God like no other. The shut ins and isolations in the bedroom, the dreadful routines of struggling to make a meal, the unhappiness that settled in me, the no desiring for food--- was real, yet I knew my God was and is realer than that. I knew I had to seek God first, so I made the conscious decision to do just that. I started going to church to learn how to be in God's Presence and surrender it all to Him.

I attended church on a regular basis for an extended period. I would write my notes, participate in service, and do my routine of living---went to work, took care of my kids, and going out as I chose to go out. After a while, I began to feel "churched out". I didn't have the desire to go to church as I did before because my routine was the same as before I went to church, yet the only difference was I heard God's Word. Not only this, I was made aware of the power that resided and resides in His Word. While I embraced my moments, life continued to happen. Some days were easy, some were tough, yet I was still numb and so heartless. I pretended and played my part to make it—I faked it to make it, yet I was still broken and felt so alone.

Reality hit!!! When my youngest daughter started understanding some things, she began to ask some questions. These questions caused responses that caused so much pain to even go back to certain moments to relive it all over again. I asked myself how am I going to explain this stuff to her when I truly haven't even touched it myself. I remember the little girl that grew up so fearful, numb, and clueless because her mother was so taken with life that questions as such couldn't be asked, nevertheless answered. I knew I owed it to my daughter to tell her the truth. It was the hard truth, yet it was my and the truth. The truth that her mother and father weren't getting back together, her mother's true story of being abused, the embracement of sin out of the experienced pain, and the mere fact that her mother needed God's help.

For me, this was scary, now I had to call my mother for help because I didn't know how to move on from that point. I coped with it, and it resulted in me getting intoxicated to the point of finding myself on my bedroom floor with a trash can by my head, not being able to lift my head up. I remember seeing my son come upon me with tears in his eyes, not saying a word. As he left out of my presence, after hearing me telling him that I was okay don't worry, tears fell instantly. I was soaked in my tears yet again, yet this time in the state of helplessness. I called out to God and pleaded for His Help! When I rose from that floor, I had strength like no other—something happened when I was on the fall and rose.

I knew I had to change. I knew I had to get it together. I knew my kids needed me even though I felt as if life had let me down. I knew I had to let go of the alcohol, partying, women, and my situationships. I had to because instantly it came to me that all I was doing was setting myself up for failure. Wisdom and understanding were settling within me, for I asked God to give me an understanding, so I could obey His Instructions and Will for my life (Psalm 119:34, NLT).

I picked up the notes I wrote from church and began to pray for an understanding. I was *led* to do that, and I did just that. This now was my ritual of living. I had to gain an understanding of The Word to apply it to my life. I was hungry and thirsty for God's Word because I knew my blessings were in me diligently seeking Him (Matthew 5:6, NLT). Going to church was a part of my routine. Before I realized it, the desire to have alcohol decreased, the partying decreased, the desire for women decreased, and the need to be or desiring a married man or situationship completely faded away.

Thank You God! I knew then that God had a plan for me for my good and not to harm me, yet instead to give me a bright future and hope (Jeremiah 29:11, NLT). Yes, God had this already set up for me. Thank You God! I looked in the mirror and realized that a change was coming upon me. It was very scary, yet I knew this change was necessary…. I knew I had to fight through my mess to be a better woman and mother. God was making me a "new" person. The old me was shedding away, and I welcomed my new beginning.

Even in the midst of me doing different things and not engaging in the old stuff I used to do—temptations were always at bay—that's when I realized that I wasn't just fighting my flesh, the enemy was present, so then I knew I was on a spiritual battlefield. I became wise to understand that it was a fight against the principalities and not the flesh (Ephesians 6:12)—it now was a spiritual thing that I knew only God could help, fight, and save me from and of. BUT

GOD! Now I was beginning to fellowship with God, and

gaining knowledge of understanding the multitude of Jesus

the Christ, The Cross, and being reassured that it is through

and by Jesus that I'm able to walk in pure victory and

intimacy with God---my God, my God (2 Corinthians 5:17-

18, NLT) . I was super excited because I was learning how to

have relations with God for myself, and I was seeing my life

changed.

Chapter 5

Letting Go: Pressing Pass the Pain

Accepting my truth, letting go of habitual behaviors and activities, and acknowledging "me"—was not easy. BUT GOD! In the midst of my life changing, I endured pain, suffering, struggle, disappointment, rejection, and uncertainties. I knew that the spiritual warfare was real, yet in the same token, I knew and know my God was and is bigger and realer than anything I would face. I knew I had to press pass all the pain with and by my faith in order for me to be healed, delivered, and set free from all I've endured in my lifetime--- I needed Jesus, my Strength and Redeemer. No other way around it! In Hebrews 11:1, NLT, it clearly identifies that *faith* shows the reality of what we hope for; it is the evidence of things we cannot see. I could not see or gain an understanding of how I would come whole, yet I trusted and trust God. This within itself was and is enough for me for me to grasp and hold on to.

My ex-husband remarried, kids older, school completed (obtained master's degree), nice home, nice car, still felt the presence of God, heard from God, yet still had a void. Where and why was there still a void when I had an intimate relationship with God? Thank you for asking---because in my mind, I was still holding on to the memories of my past. Day in and day out, I couldn't understand why me? Why did I have to be that little girl who through the years conditioned her mind to forget her childhood? Why me? Why did I have to be sexually abused or raped by the first guy I dealt with in high school? Why me? Why did my first daughter's father abuse me physically, mentally, and emotionally just because he was jealous and insecure? Why me? Why did a guy that I always admired choose to marry me over all the other girls he dated? Why me? Why did the only man I truly ever loved, why did he turn to be a reminder of the men that hurt my mother in the past? Why me? Why did I have to get abused, yet hid it to the world as if all was well for the sake of saving a marriage that was already over when he first put his hands on me? Why did I stay? Why did I even want it to work? Why me? Why was I desiring only a touch from a woman? Why me? Why did I choose to be with married or taken men? Why me? Why did I become addicted to gin and sex? Why me? Why was looking in the mirror of that same little girl a mere reflection of the woman I've become as a mother of three, divorced, and struggling to survive? Why me?

I dealt with all of this every day, every day, every day, BUT I knew God for myself. As I reflect to my journal with an entry from January 29, 2019, my exact words were: 'Lord, I need you right now. Within my heart, it is breaking into a million tiny pieces. All I'm hearing and feeling is affliction-affliction-affliction. God, Your Word says, even though I feel this/afflictions, Lord, You are bigger than them. In Your Word, You remind me that those of the righteous are afflicted, yet You will deliver us from them all.' As I journaled, I also heard from God, and was led by the Holy Spirit, so still on this specified day as I journaled, I wrote, 'Now You're telling me to rest in You Lord.'

As I was looking for the Scripture, I came across Psalm 37: "Rest in the Lord," the verses that highlighted spiritually to me were-→vv 5, 7 [v5: Commit everything you do to the Lord. Trust him, and he will help you. v7: Be still in the presence of the Lord, and wait patiently for him to act. Don't worry about evil people who prosper or fret about their wicked schemes].' On the side bar, I wrote *v.11 (done something to me), v.16 (my God), and v.25, so as I reference these verses from NLT, v.11 reads *The lowly will possess the land will live in peace and prosperity.* The Bible notation for explanation stated that in v.11 The Lord is the author of **peace** he brings peace to a chaotic world. His wisdom guides the *lowly* into the way of peace (998). Therefore, v.16 reads *it is better to be godly and have little than to be evil and rich,* and v.25 reads *once I was young, and now that I am old, yet I have never seen the godly abandoned or their children begging for bread.* So therefore, after I journaled vv 5, 7, I continued to write, 'Read the entire scripture is what the Spirit gave me. So, I'm doing just that. Thank You Lord.

Still focusing on my journal entry, it further read '***Holy Spirit:*** Do not fret, stay focus in your worship and praise. The devil is a liar. You're winning. Study your fruit you're producing. Keep focus on The Lord. Distractions coming. You have to stay steadfast on your call. Do not stay in the brokenness and affliction. You have the authority to trample over your enemies or any principalities. Operate in your authority. Fret not! You will not be moved. DO NOT LOSE FOCUS! Nothing else matters. Trust me, when you can't see it! {**Now God begun to speak to me**}: Faith—press pass the pain!!Press and keep pressing. Don't give up. Stay still & trust me. I AM BIGGER! You have me, why are you worried? Cast all your worries upon me…Be happy

now! ---*God*

After receipt of all of that harmonized with and in my

moment of why's and pain, I had to let go. No other way

around it! But then I pondered on how do I let go, what is the

process of letting go...So did that mean I had to let go of my

love I had, the coping mechanism I learned and conditioned

myself with, did I truly have to go back to the "darkness"

again---No way! That familiar feeling came over me once

again, yet this time, it was different—God assured me that

He had me. Instantly within my Spirit these two verses came

to mind, and I spoke them out loud:

> ***Psalm 121:1-2, KJV:*** I will lift up mine eyes unto the
>
> hills, from whence cometh my help. My help cometh
>
> from the LORD, which made heaven and earth. **AND**

Psalm 91: 4, KJV: He shall cover thee with his feathers, and under his wings shalt thou trust: his truth shall be thy shield and buckler [armor and protection].

Thank You Lord!

Life happened, so now being that I transitioned my churches under new leadership, I began to gain so much more wisdom, confidence in God, and developing a newfound intimate relationship with God. One of my God encountering, and memorable moments occurred on February 5, 2019. I journaled this moment that read: 'Day 3 of corporate fasting: As I walked on my last lap, I felt 'opposition of pain' –my knees began aching, my calves began to burn in the back, and I started to breathe more rapidly as I continuously told myself, this is your last lap, you're almost home, so keep pressing. The moment I told myself that, the Holy Spirit instructed me to look down—as I stumbled across what I saw, God said that the needed steps back are necessary to get it, and, but keep pressing. It was a "feather". As I picked up this feather; I vividly remember

hearing God say to me:

See in life things will place you in the "opposition of pain", yet remember I will keep you under my wings and give you strength. You must press pass the pain and opposition to obtain your reward in the end. Not only this, the pressing and sacrifice is greater than the pain of the and from the opposition. You must finish to understand the outcome—Press pass the resistance, opposition, and the pain no matter how bad it hurts; how tough it may seem. Look up to the hills which cometh your help, it comes from me. All in the due season, you shall reap it all abundantly **if you** faint not. It's all about pressing pass the pain. ------------------------- *God* '

**As I referenced the "feather", please be mindful that I love

feathers. Why? When I fully surrendered to God's Will and

not my own, I started randomly finding feathers when I was

at my lowest, darkest, and hopeless moments. When I saw a

feather, I felt as if God literally had me under his wings,

therefore the above message is very powerful because I was

seeing these things being applied and manifested in my life.

I referenced Psalm 91:4 after my encounter with God. See what the Holy Spit kept telling me was that God is so strategic in His thoughts and plans for me, that He will make sure I have a future and hope despite of the journey that will have afflictions, oppositions, disappointments, etc., yet **I** must consciously and mentally make the decision to press pass the pain of opposition. I knew that I had to go back to this little girl filled with so much "darkness" and introduce her to the "light" that I found by letting go and pressing pass my pain. God's Word gave and reminded me of the assurance that I would be okay when I go back to touch my past that was left unkept simply by God being my light in my most sentimental, tough, fearful, and loneliness of my "darkness"---Isaiah 42:16, NLT reads *I will lead blind Israel down a new path, guiding them along an unfamiliar way. I will brighten the darkness before them and smooth out the road ahead of them. Yes, I will indeed do these things; I will not forsake them.*

From this I gathered that all that I'd endured was necessary for my purpose. It was about experiencing things in life that were meant to destroy my light, yet I found Jesus My Savior deep down in my dark moments, and He was and is my light to shine. Not only this, I surrendered and told Him that I couldn't do anything without Him, and that I needed Him to give me strength to overcome that darkness".

The "darkness" that lived in my past/childhood that I was so afraid to touch which caused me to be numb most of my life. Why? The painful memories attached to it---the little girl in the corner filled with darkness. Now that I have my light, my God, I knew I was ready and prepared spiritually to go back to face the pain.

Chapter 6

Going Back to Face the Pain-Forgiveness

Before even knowing that God would grant my desires of writing a book about my life, I never knew that I had to go back to face the pain of "my darkness". BUT GOD knew it was necessary! Before starting in this chapter, I must enlighten you on my experience that occurred when God told me it was time to write the book, and I had to go back to relive the moments of my "darkness". I knew I could talk with God and receive an answer because this is the bond that we have. So, on March 5, 2019 at 1:36am, God woke me up to do the preliminary sketching of the book contents/outline.

When I prepared to begin, the Holy Spirit led me to a page on social media, and I ran across a shirt that read, "Straight Outta Darkness—whoever believes John 3:16". I was like WOW God, You are so amazing, WOW! You just did that! So, as I meditated, it is a familiar Scripture, *For*

God so loved the world that He gave His only begotten Son, that whoever believes in Him should not perish but have everlasting life (John 3:16, NKJV). So, then, me still saying WOW God, I desired more. God led me to v.21 that reads *But he who does the truth comes to the light, that his deeds may be clearly seen, that they have been done in God.* At this moment, I was blown away because with me knowing of, having a relationship with, believing in my heart, and confessing Jesus as my Savior, I was like you know what God, You got me. Not only do you have me, you have made me new, cleaned me up, and molded my character so people can see you as my light from shining within. With me knowing this, saying this, guess what---tears dropped as I began thinking about reliving my past to go back to face the pain.

As I journaled on March 5, 2019, I wrote, 'As I began to pray to God because instantly I told Him that I was afraid to go back and live these moments, God said, "It's time for your full deliverance. I've given you all that you need. It's time to reap your blessings. Give me the glory in it all. Look at the right, allow that to be your start.' Well, what was to my right that God was referencing? I have a wall décor with crosses and the main words on the crosses are **Serenity Prayer, Faith, & Bless.** I told God, You are so amazing! From that point, it was easy to start and importantly being prepared for this chapter because it reveals my true "darkness" of pain.

Before I tapped into my truth, I had to recall that God is true to His Promises and The Word are real—*It is the same with my word, I send it out, and it always produces fruit. It will accomplish all I want it to, and it will prosper everywhere I send it (Isaiah 55:11, NLT)* –so if God told me that He will know the plans He has for me and declares plans to prosper me and not harm, plans to give me hope and a future—here again Jeremiah 29:11. I knew that I could walk in my past, and my steps be ordered by God. It's more evident when focusing on Hebrews 4:12-13, NLT, *For the word of God is alive and powerful. It is sharper than the sharpest two-edged sword, cutting between soul and spirit, between joint and marrow. It exposes our innermost thoughts and desires. Nothing in all creation is hidden from God. Everything is naked and exposed before his eyes, and he is the one to whom we are accountable*. My God, my God, my God—I pray you catch this as I did! So, if God knows and He holds me accountable, then I had to come to terms with the underlying cause of my truth that lied in the "darkness" of this little girl that lived life as it happened by numbing her pain, taking the numerous blows, allowing life to happen, yet in a position to be ready to face the "darkness" of her ultimate brokenness.

As I wrote the last sentence above, I declared and decreed deliverance, healing, and liberty from the memories and pain associated with the "darkness" solely by my faith that it is done in Jesus Name. My darkness was the fact that the little girl that you read about in the corner with the tears soaking in her pants was indeed me—I was molested by a family member at the age of four. During my spiritual journey, I identified the roots, exposed the roots, and God killed the roots associated with this hurt, pain, and pure "darkness" that hovered over me for 34 years of my life. Being spiritually aware based on the acquired knowledge, the molestation created strongholds to keep me in bondage which consisted of the Dumb and Deaf Spirit (persistent crying), Spirit of Infirmity (weakness), Spirit of Fear (anxiety, stress; lack of trust, doubt), Perverse Spirit (incest: molestation), Spirit of Whoredoms (worldliness), and Spirit of Heaviness (inner hurt, torn spirit, broken heart, heaviness)—6 Spirits that created the stronghold that originated from being molested that manifested within me for 34 years to produce *A Past Left Unkept*. I will not go into details about these Spirits, yet just know they are real and exist, and necessary when seeking revelation from the stronghold identification when dismantling them in order for one to be set free, healed, and delivered.

I remember when I was ready to uncover the "darkness" of molestation, God showed me what happened in the form of a black and white movie. The movie revealed me seeing my mother leave me to go to work and leaving me in the care of someone she trusted. I saw me looking at my mother's car tail lights as she went down the long dirt path and crying my heart out. Then immediately, I would go in the little dark and lonely room crying. Instantly, I felt from what God showed, the sense of hoping he wasn't in the mood to touch me. I often cried so hard that he would give up and just leave me there. I remember touching my genital area, and telling my sibling it hurt, and just cry. ***Help me Lord, I need You right now…Tears are rolling down my face as I write this—Thank You God for staying right here with me… [Pause Break Needed] *** I prayed for him to stop. I prayed, I prayed—not realizing then what I was doing when my tears ran down my little cheeks. But it kept happening, until my mother was informed. I remember he got sent away, but it was still strange and felt awkward because I've seen a picture of me being in the photo when going to visit him with the family. This man took me away from me before I was able to understand life. This man took away my innocence and opened me up to the subjection of a cold world. This man made my life a living hell before my steps in life were even fulfilled—4 years old! Yet this was my life.

Now, is this the many reasons why I couldn't trust anyone around my kids? Is this why I had to have my husband tell me what he was going to do before touching me? Is this why I cannot take someone being so close to me? Is this why I doubt love? Is this the cause of many failed friendships and relationships? God, all this was purposed, right?

In the process of my life happening, especially during my transformation process and pressing pass the pain stages, God dealt with my heart centered on this aspect, being molested, in my life. God began to show me my life from His perspective. It resembled something like this to give me a sense of understanding:

- o Little girl—Molested at age of 4
- o 6-13 years old – Witness of abuse
- o 14 years old- Raped
- o 15-16 years old- Became pregnant
- o 17-20 years old- Life happened
- o 20 years old- 2nd child came along
- o 21-23 years old – Life happened
- o 24 years old- Marriage
- o 24-26 years old- Life happened, and 3rd child came
- o 27-33 years old- Promiscuous Life Style and Depression
- o 34-37 years old- Promiscuous Life Style, reignited church life while experiencing life challenges.
- o 38 years old- Made up mind to break the cycle

Through the overview of my life, I kept myself in bondage because I did not want to forgive this man that caused me so much pain. It became evident why my guards were up and also why I wouldn't allow people to get close to me. Also, why my husband had to be guided when handling me, why I guarded my kids when this man would come around. Because I had been violated at such a very, very, very young age. Furthermore, I started questioning this forgiveness thing. If I was thinking about having to forgive this man, what about the other people that were attached to some sort of experienced pain, rejection, and abandonment in my life—my mother, these guys, some associates, my ex-husband—what about them God?

God gracefully answered, "You must forgive because I forgive you." Now, that I was at a place in desiring more of the Word, I had to find Scripture to help me apply this in my life, so the Holy Spirit gave me Ephesians 4:31-32, NLT, *Get rid of all bitterness, rage, anger, harsh words, and slander, as well as types of evil behavior. v.32 Instead, be kind to each other, tenderhearted, forgiving one another, just as God through Christ has forgiven you.* I read this and was like WOW, I must forgive. If God forgives me, I must forgive them. God gave me strength to ask questions, to express how I felt, and for me to say, I forgive you to everyone that caused me affliction or opposition that resulted in my experienced pain. Importantly, I learned during this process that when I became afflicted and offended; it was my choice to be that way. God tells us in The Word that the afflictions and oppositions, a part of life that we will endure, shall happen, but we will not be consumed. Therefore, here I lived all these years, choosing to be a prisoner of my pain. Yet, when I understood and FORGAVE; this feeling of release was and still is unexplainable.

I thank God for these moments because He gracefully, intentionally, and strategically prepared me in my brokenness to go back to every aspect of pain in my life and forgive. My deliverance, healing, and the liberty were bounded up in my forgiveness. As soon as I forgave, I did not see any "darkness" around that little girl anymore. God, by His light, set me free. It was necessary for me to go back to the past that was left unkept.

Chapter 7

The End: A Past That God Allowed Me to Touch- My Past Now Kept by Faith

When I saw the light of God overcome the darkness that was dwelling in my life for 34 years, tears ran down my face. All I could do was worship and give God all the praise and glory. Did you ever imagine or even think that unforgiveness would or could alter your whole life if not done? I'm proof that it could and is possible, BUT GOD. I grew up in church as a young girl, yet routinely went with my mother and grandmother because it was the right thing to do. Life happened. Darkness overcome my life in ways that caused me to press through solely by being numb to the pain. Until I grew weary, in the state of depression, and knew my lifestyle after my divorce would kill me or hurt someone else; I knew my life had to change. There was a strong thirst that filled my entire being that was only after God's heart and His Will.

I needed what God has only if I seek Him first—nothing else really mattered or matters.

I found the light of my salvation, light of my peace, and the ultimate light of my everything—God. As my relationship became more intimate with God, my faith increased tremendously. It was by faith that I trusted and trust God, so God knew I was prepared holistically to go back to my past to acknowledge and accept it, so He could heal, deliver, and set me free from the "darkness" and all the pain I'd endured from it. Importantly, based on the obtained knowledge, wisdom, and understanding from my spiritual transformation, renewed mind, and new heart, I had to learn that forgiveness is necessary. Why and how does anyone forgive? Forgiveness is a must because once one does it, you're no longer the captive of or to the situation or the individual any longer. In other words, you only make yourself a prisoner to the affliction or offense by beating yourself up because of you holding on the pain associated with it. Instead, the moment you forgive is the moment in which you release yourself from the bondages, burdens, and heartaches that you release back to God. God is the vengeance, so He will fight the battle for you. You must forgive as God forgives us. For the Word of God is alive and powerful (Hebrews 4:12, NLT). So therefore, we must always remember, *But when you are praying, first forgive anyone you are holding a grudge against, so that your Father in heaven will forgive your sins too (Mark 11:25, NLT)*. WOW! So, with this being God's Word, we must forgive. Ask yourself, is it really worth going through the dark moments, pain, resentment, isolation, etc.? I can sincerely answer that question; it is not worth it! Life happens. Things happens. God is real & He saves, and HE IS THE LIGHT IN OUR DARKEST MOMENTS! Not me, you, your sister, your brother, your mother, your father, your Pastor, or even your spouse—GOD IS!

If you've experienced something similar, haven't forgiven someone who violated you, hurt, or caused you to lose a part of you; I will encourage you to seek forgiveness. I pray that you are grounded in a support system in which you can embrace your hard truth, build an intimate relationship with God—"your light", allow God to order your steps, so you also can be healed, delivered, and set free. You are not a victim of what you been through or going through: **You are a Victor and more than a Conqueror!**

The moment I took myself out of the equation and replaced it with God, my life immediately changed. God already knew my life would be as it was and as it is, yet I had to surrender it all, even the control mentality, and trust God. Based on my spiritual discipline and God continuing to work on my character, I was God's Ambassador going back in the enemy's territory and getting my pure happiness and joy back. Not only that, I found my self-worth and innocence there as well—Yes, I took that also—God told me to get it all! ☺ It was by my faith that I knew I could do just that because I knew and know its Christ who strengthens me, so no matter what I had to encounter, it was time to go back to my "dark" past with my "light"---God by my side. God allowed my past to be kept simply with a touch by my faith. I hoped and prayed for light in my dark place, and the outcome of putting it all behind—memories and the pain—it was by faith that this came to past even when I couldn't begin to see it manifest as I pondered about going back to get my stuff---BUT GOD DID!

It took me 34 years to have the desire to go back to my past, simply because I was so afraid to face the "darkness" of my truth that resonated behind and in it, and not being aware of the power of forgiveness. It took my wilderness experience of life happening, being under true leadership, prayers, God's Word, obedience, being in God's Presence, forming and having an intimate relationship with God, and the actual pain for me to face the reality of the need to go back to my past. The actual pain from my "darkness" **had to**

be present for me to have the thirsting desire for light to

overcome it---God, so that I could learn how to keep my past

as part of my journey, yet allowing God's Grace and love to

be sufficient enough only by a touch of faith to move on, and

walk gracefully in my divine purpose. I am no longer a

victim of molestation, abuse, depression, and rejection—I

AM AN OVERCOMER who was able to overcome a dark

past that was left unkept....

Conclusion

Now that God has led me to go back to my past that was left unkept, I have forgiven all the individuals, and now I am FREE! What lies next? Great question! Now, it is really time to embrace God's transformation as I embark the next chapters of my life…What a minute, life is still happening in this transformation process! Do I go back to the comfort place that was in my past—that familiarity of numbness? Do I press on? How do I keep pressing when life really has me down at this very moment? Is it really happening again? Is there a difference of how I perceive things now since I have gone back and dealt with my past, or is it the same thing happening over and over again—the cycles? One thing for sure and two things for certain, I am not going back to the comfort of my past. I know now in my maturity that I must keep pressing and moving forward. Yes, life is still happening to me even though I have a made-up mind! There is a difference....

Now, the BIG difference is in the way I am perceiving things, people, situations, and any encounter that approaches me as I compare it to where I was in my past. I refuse to go back and have pity parties about happenings of my past; I refuse to allow negativity to invade in my space; and importantly, I now release all my worries, burdens, and uncertainties back to God. I am focused on doing what is necessary for The Kingdom. It's not about me at the end of the day; it is about you, you, and you, yet most importantly and foremost, it is all about glorifying God.

God has and is continuing to equip me for a time such as this. Life is truly happening, yet I have made up in my mind that *my purpose is greater than my past*. Therefore, as I journeyed back to my reality after going back to my past, I now know that ALL that God allowed me to endure was absolutely necessary for a time such as this. A time such as this exemplifies moments of seeing others do as they please, having to stay in the home to study, interceding in prayer for others, turning down temptations, accepting the fact of my truth that I just feel awkward in certain places and around certain people, more afflictions, oppositions, etc. are happening. But wait; doesn't it supposed to get a little easier now. What do you do when the battle chooses you?

One begins to think and say, "BUT GOD, I have surrendered it all and now I'm on your Team, yet it still feels as if I am fighting." Guess what? You are, yet in The Word, it tells us that we will not have to fight this battle; we must take our rightful place, trust God as we rest in Him, and God will give deliverance to us (2 Chronicles 20:17, KJV). Therefore, the battles shall and will come, yet the million-dollar question is— How does one prepare himself for the battles in life as it is happening? Great question, thank you for asking! God has given me the wisdom to assist you in answering this profound question. Let's ponder for a second with a quick scenario.

Jill is a 20-year old female that recently got engaged to Thomas. Jill was raised in a single-parent household in which she is the only child, rarely saw her mother due to her mother being the sole provider of the household and works in a fast-food restaurant to help her mother out the best she can. Jill is active in her church—youth leader. Jill is also pregnant. Thomas on the other end was raised in a two-parent home, parents owned their trucking company, and he is the Co-CEO of their family-owned business. Thomas just asked Jill to move out of her mother's home with him, so they can live as a family. Jill is very hesitant on making this move as Thomas is puzzled to why because this is all she talked about.

Let's pause for a second and discuss some things not mentioned as we solely focus on Jill and her current household. Jill's uncle, Lee, has been staying with them for three months due to him being evicted out of his home, and her mother wanting to help her brother until he gets back on his feet. Since Lee moved in, Thomas noticed that Jill has become very withdrawn from him and her friends, been watching a lot of pornography, does not desire to kiss him as she did before, made numerous threats on resigning her church leadership role due to feelings of unworthiness, does not get her hair and nails done anymore, and gets very frustrated when Lee's name is mentioned. Hmmm…now you are thinking—Something has happened to Jill, but what?

If you have not noticed, before Jill's uncle, Lee, came to live with them, Jill appeared to be enjoying life, and then suddenly Jill's behaviors and responses changed. Not only that—Who has Jill become? She is not the same individual that we initially read about; something in life happened. But what? Little did Jill's mother and Thomas know, that every day for the past three months when Jill would come home after work, her uncle Lee would molest and rape her. Jill was three months pregnant. Wait, isn't that the amount of time Lee has been staying there? Absolutely! Now, not only is Jill harboring the fact that she has been molested and raped and all the feelings, emotions, hurt, and pain attached with it; she now is carrying her uncle's child, engaged to a man that she loves in which he thinks this is his child, and Lee is her mother's only brother. Now what? Life happened? Life is happening? Jill is stuck! The battle chose her!

This scenario reminds me of my life, as you read in *A Past Left Unkept*, BUT GOD equips us to identify the root of our problems, issues, and happenings. Not only does He equips us, He teaches us essential tools that we can use daily as we face the principalities, powers, rulers of the darkness, and spiritual wickedness of such a cold, cold, cold world. He even cares and loves us so much that He has given us the apostolic authority and power to cast down the strongholds that try to bind us in our lives as it did in the above scenario to Jill. Therefore, take a journey with me in Volume 2 of *A*

Past Left Unkept to be informed on how to tackle the battles when life happens to you. It is not an easy task, yet as God reassures us in His Word: *We can do all things through Christ who strengthens us* (Philippians 4:13, KJV). Let us put on the whole armor of God—Helmet of Salvation, Breastplate of Righteousness, Sword of the Spirit, Shield of Faith, Belt of Truth, and the Gospel of Peace (Ephesians 6:11-18)--- as we continue on our journey while life is happening to us.

You do not have to remain a prisoner of your past! You do not have to remain a victim! You do not have to live stuck for years over hidden secrecies, disappointments, hurt, pain—You do not because when God sets us free, we are free indeed (John 8:36, KJV)! By the wisdom, apostolic power and authority God has invested in me, I will show you how to press on, why it is essential for you to keep it moving and not allowing yourself the chance of getting stuck, and learning how to live when life is happening after you have went back to touch a past left unkept as the battles continue

to choose you. The process begins in your mind—Ask

yourself, Am I ready to stop these cycles? Am I willing,

ready, and able to stop the generational curses? Aren't I

worthy enough to enjoy life without having to feel the

constant agony of pain, disappointment, etc.? You are

worthy, and *A Past Left Unkept, Part Two* will provide you

with inspiration to keep moving beyond your past while you

embrace your now while preparing for your future simply by

a touch by faith, praying, and staying in God's Presence.